SCHOLASTIC

40 CROSS-NUMBER PUZZLES

Multiplication & Division

BY BOB OLENYCH

New York • Toronto • London • Auckland • Sydney
Mexico City • New Delhi • Hong Kong • Buenos Aires

Teaching *Resources*

To all the students who enjoy the fun and challenge of math.

Cover design by Maria Lilja
Cover illustration by Dave Clegg
Interior design by Melinda Belter

ISBN 0-439-51879-2

Copyright © 2004 by Bob Olenych. All rights reserved.
Printed in the U.S.A.

2 3 4 5 6 7 8 9 10   40   11 10 09 08 07 06 05 04

40
CROSS-NUMBER PUZZLES
CONTENTS

40 CROSS-NUMBER PUZZLES INTRODUCTION

MULTIPLICATION AND DIVISION PRACTICE CAN BE FUN!

If fluency and accuracy are the goals you have established for your students learning multiplication and division, then they should partake in regular review and practice with these skills. The key to motivating students is to provide them with a variety of activities that are interesting and stimulating. To support my students as they gain fluency and accuracy, I have created skill-building practice puzzles that they really enjoy.

WHAT YOU'LL FIND IN THIS BOOK

This book offers a collection of 40 multiplication and division activities for a broad range of skills and abilities. The puzzles begin with multiplication, then progress to division. Within each skill section, they are arranged from easy to difficult. You can match the needs of your students and target a specific skill by checking the detailed skill description, listed both in the Table of Contents and on each activity page.

Some highlights of this book include the activities that reinforce two skills—expressing written numbers as standard numbers, then multiplying them. For example, if a problem asks students to multiply seven hundred sixty-four by five hundred thirteen, students must first express the written numbers as standard numbers, then multiply them. You can assign this type of activity at any time during the school year, as it serves as an excellent review of these two skills.

HOW TO USE THIS BOOK

Be sure to use these puzzles in a way that best suits the needs of your class. You may find it helpful to assign certain puzzles as practice work to follow a lesson, as in-class review work, or as homework. Where necessary, be sure to remind students that if they need more room to compute, they can use the back of the sheet or a piece of scrap paper—depending on your class policy. Whether they are solving a riddle or determining the place value of a number, students are motivated to check each problem so that they can finish the puzzle successfully.

CONNECTIONS TO THE MATH STANDARDS

Most of the puzzles in this book target NCTM 2000 objectives listed under the Number and Operations standard. These objectives include understanding ways to represent numbers, determining meanings of operations and how they relate to one another, and computing with fluency and accuracy. This book is packed with exercises that require students to use the operations of multiplication and division in a variety of formats.

I am confident that your students, like mine, will enjoy this collection of puzzles and reap the benefits of practicing these essential skills.

Bob Olenych

| 1 DIGIT X 3 DIGITS | Solve the problems and write your answers in the appropriate across and down positions. |

ACROSS

1. $581 \times 5 =$

4. $447 \times 8 =$

7. $993 \times 7 =$

9. $848 \times 9 =$

10. $715 \times 9 =$

11. $832 \times 5 =$

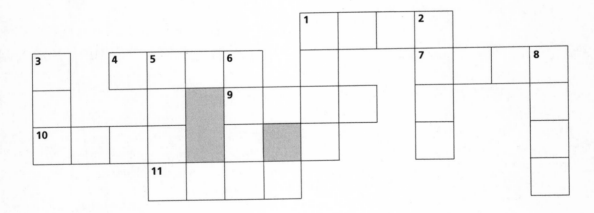

DOWN

1. $339 \times 6 =$

2. $947 \times 6 =$

3. $438 \times 2 =$

5. $606 \times 9 =$

6. $968 \times 7 =$

8. $377 \times 3 =$

CROSS-NUMBER
2
PUZZLE

1 DIGIT X 3 DIGITS

Solve the problems and write your answers in the appropriate across and down positions.

ACROSS

1. 475
      × 9

3. 432
      × 7

5. 841
      × 2

7. 969
      × 2

8. 682
      × 7

10. 842
       × 6

12. 317
       × 6

DOWN

2. 716
      × 8

3. 394
      × 9

4. 792
      × 4

6. 729
      × 3

9. 956
      × 5

10. 962
       × 6

11. 274
       × 8

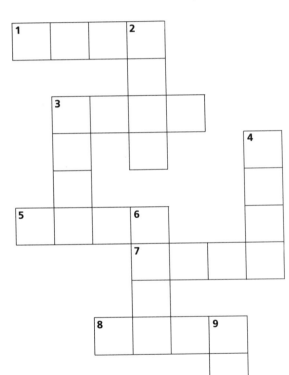

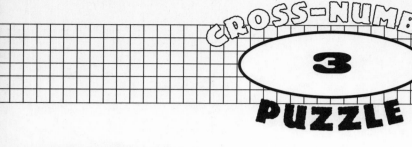

CROSS-NUMBER 3 PUZZLE

| 1 DIGIT X 4 DIGITS | Solve the problems and write your answers in the appropriate across and down positions. |

ACROSS

2. $8{,}936 \times 8 =$

3. $8{,}407 \times 7 =$

6. $3{,}715 \times 6 =$

7. $2{,}938 \times 4 =$

9. $7{,}521 \times 9 =$

11. $4{,}355 \times 5 =$

DOWN

1. $4{,}824 \times 8 =$

4. $9{,}080 \times 9 =$

5. $5{,}006 \times 2 =$

8. $6{,}049 \times 3 =$

9. $9{,}447 \times 7 =$

10. $1{,}967 \times 5 =$

M
U
L
T
I
P
L
I
C
A
T
I
O
N

2 DIGITS X 2 DIGITS   Solve the problems and write your answers in the appropriate across and down positions.

ACROSS

2.   59
       × 36

3.   83
       × 94

5.   88
       × 98

7.   44
       × 49

9.   51
       × 79

11.   67
        × 60

13.   23
        × 55

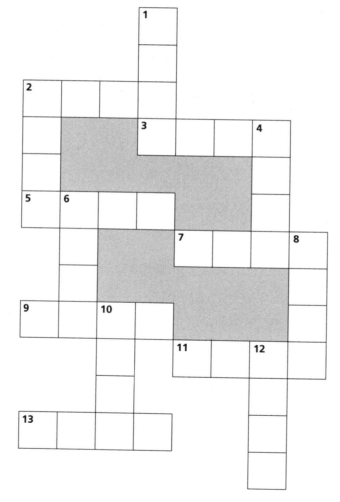

DOWN

1.   39
       × 73

2.   28
       × 81

4.   45
       × 47

6.   74
       × 85

8.   90
       × 75

10.   37
        × 68

12.   96
        × 25

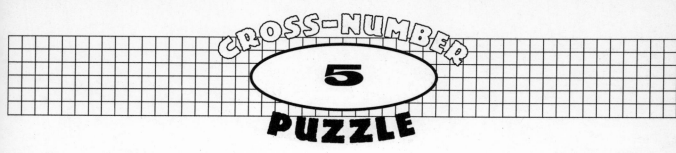

| 2 DIGITS X 3 DIGITS | Solve the problems and write your answers in the appropriate across and down positions. |

ACROSS

2. 592 × 32 =

5. 288 × 39 =

6. 333 × 82 =

8. 717 × 84 =

9. 749 × 76 =

10. 863 × 90 =

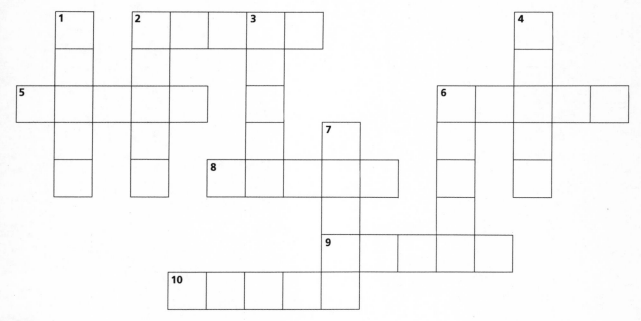

DOWN

1. 206 × 59 =

2. 398 × 46 =

3. 634 × 75 =

4. 505 × 74 =

6. 424 × 63 =

7. 910 × 25 =

CROSS-NUMBER **6** PUZZLE

2 DIGITS X 3 DIGITS Solve the problems and write your answers in the appropriate across and down positions.

ACROSS

3. $247 \times 63 =$

5. $448 \times 82 =$

7. $958 \times 29 =$

9. $400 \times 66 =$

11. $517 \times 88 =$

12. $340 \times 42 =$

DOWN

1. $706 \times 45 =$

2. $659 \times 32 =$

4. $568 \times 94 =$

6. $375 \times 76 =$

8. $986 \times 26 =$

10. $832 \times 57 =$

2 DIGITS X 4 DIGITS   Solve the problems and write your answers in the appropriate across and down positions.

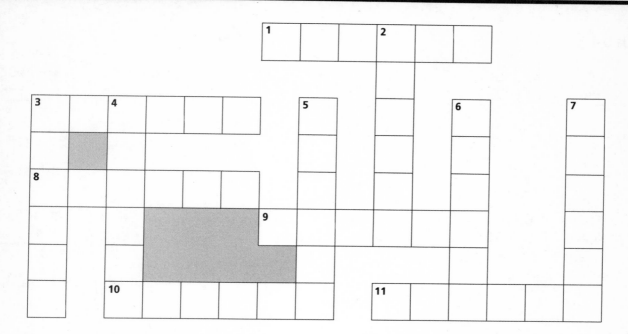

ACROSS

1. 6,435
  × 58

3. 6,340
  × 68

8. 2,506
  × 42

9. 8,321
  × 37

10. 2,090
  × 97

11. 9,174
  × 78

DOWN

2. 3,472
  × 84

3. 7,807
  × 63

4. 2,406
  × 52

5. 4,760
  × 29

6. 5,165
  × 41

7. 7,318
  × 94

MULTIPLICATION

| 3 DIGITS X 3 DIGITS | Solve the problems and write your answers in the appropriate across and down positions. |

ACROSS

2. 663
× 336

4. 843
× 794

6. 874
× 747

9. 582
× 548

10. 816
× 756

11. 650
× 493

DOWN

1. 299
× 299

2. 971
× 256

3. 992
× 838

5. 903
× 840

7. 765
× 302

8. 739
× 269

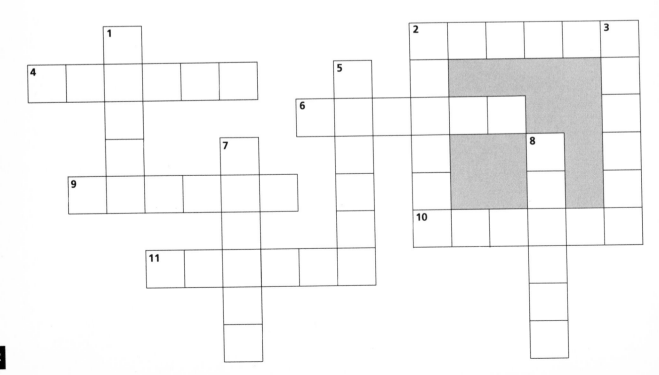

3 DIGITS X 3 DIGITS | Solve the problems and write your answers in the appropriate across and down positions.

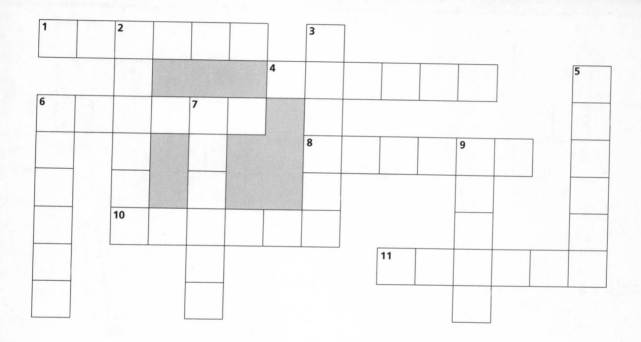

ACROSS

1. $303 \times 612 =$

4. $420 \times 937 =$

6. $580 \times 804 =$

8. $484 \times 546 =$

10. $931 \times 823 =$

11. $747 \times 250 =$

DOWN

2. $629 \times 853 =$

3. $651 \times 753 =$

5. $899 \times 560 =$

6. $915 \times 477 =$

7. $373 \times 731 =$

9. $219 \times 319 =$

MULTIPLICATION

CROSS-NUMBER 10 PUZZLE

1 DIGIT X 3 DIGITS   Solve the problems below and write your answers in the appropriate across and down positions. The number you record in the outlined box shows where the letter should go in the code boxes at the bottom to solve the riddle.

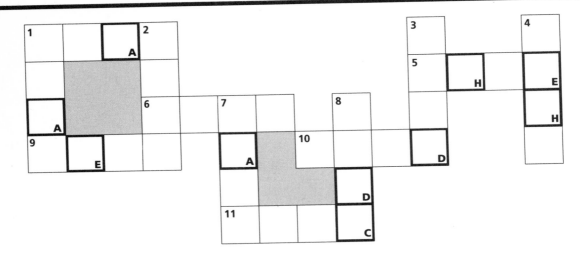

ACROSS

1. 826
  × 2

6. 607
  × 8

10. 581
  × 6

5. 870
  × 5

9. 808
  × 8

11. 694
  × 7

DOWN

1. 369
  × 4

3. 937
  × 8

7. 732
  × 7

2. 948
  × 3

4. 299
  × 7

8. 492
  × 9

What can't you give a person who has laughed his head off?

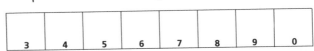

A B

CROSS-NUMBER **11** PUZZLE

2 DIGITS X 3 DIGITS

Solve the problems below and write your answers in the appropriate across and down positions. The number you record in the outlined box shows where the letter should go in the code boxes at the bottom to solve the riddle.

ACROSS

2. 560
    × 54

3. 760
    × 53

5. 847
    × 49

7. 625
    × 38

8. 909
    × 85

11. 408
    × 36

DOWN

1. 863
    × 64

2. 778
    × 50

4. 599
    × 47

6. 691
    × 45

9. 963
    × 72

10. 374
    × 29

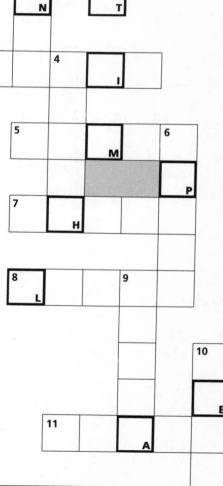

How do you contact giant squid?

| 1 | 2 | 3 | 4 | 5 | 6 | 7 | 8 | 9 | 0 |

3 DIGITS X 3 DIGITS   Solve the problems below and write your answers in the appropriate across and down positions. The number you record in the outlined box shows where the letter should go in the code boxes at the bottom to solve the riddle.

ACROSS

| **1.** 678
× 558 | **4.** 793
× 648 | **7.** 834
× 800 | **8.** 503
× 439 | **9.** 634
× 840 | **10.** 835
× 406 |

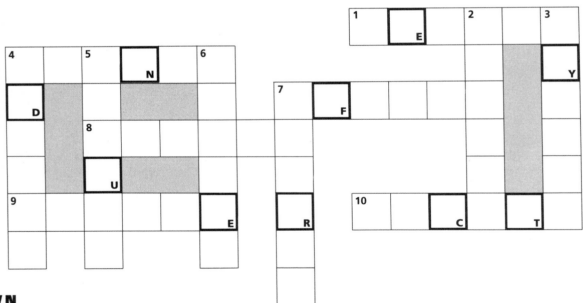

DOWN

| **2.** 600
× 584 | **3.** 470
× 968 | **4.** 948
× 572 | **5.** 793
× 482 | **6.** 781
× 600 | **7.** 937
× 724 |

What runs around a graveyard but does not move?

A S [1] [2] [3] [4] [5]   [6] [7] [8] [9] [0]

CROSS-NUMBER 13 PUZZLE

2 DIGITS X 2 DIGITS: ONES THROUGH THOUSANDS   Solve the problems below. Study your answer and fill in the puzzle by spelling out the number found in the indicated place value column (ONES, TENS, HUNDREDS, or THOUSANDS).

ACROSS

1. TENS

$$\begin{array}{r} 38 \\ \times\ 39 \\ \hline \end{array}$$

4. HUNDREDS

$$\begin{array}{r} 58 \\ \times\ 42 \\ \hline \end{array}$$

6. ONES

$$\begin{array}{r} 77 \\ \times\ 61 \\ \hline \end{array}$$

8. THOUSANDS

$$\begin{array}{r} 67 \\ \times\ 53 \\ \hline \end{array}$$

9. TENS

$$\begin{array}{r} 32 \\ \times\ 29 \\ \hline \end{array}$$

10. HUNDREDS

$$\begin{array}{r} 38 \\ \times\ 27 \\ \hline \end{array}$$

DOWN

2. ONES

$$\begin{array}{r} 77 \\ \times\ 59 \\ \hline \end{array}$$

3. THOUSANDS

$$\begin{array}{r} 93 \\ \times\ 89 \\ \hline \end{array}$$

4. HUNDREDS

$$\begin{array}{r} 64 \\ \times\ 56 \\ \hline \end{array}$$

5. THOUSANDS

$$\begin{array}{r} 48 \\ \times\ 37 \\ \hline \end{array}$$

7. HUNDREDS

$$\begin{array}{r} 95 \\ \times\ 63 \\ \hline \end{array}$$

9. HUNDREDS

$$\begin{array}{r} 79 \\ \times\ 67 \\ \hline \end{array}$$

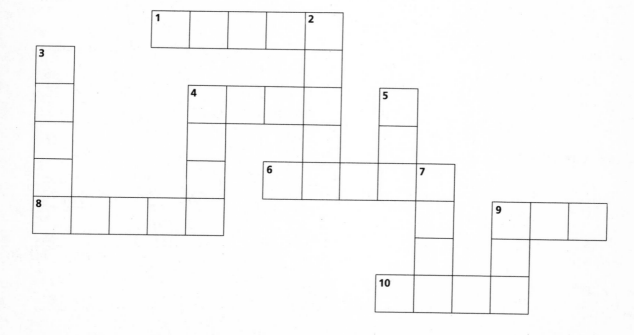

CROSS-NUMBER 14 PUZZLE

2 DIGITS X 3 DIGITS: ONES THROUGH TEN THOUSANDS

Solve the problems below. Study your answer and fill in the puzzle by spelling out the number found in the indicated place value column (ONES, TENS, HUNDREDS, THOUSANDS, or TEN THOUSANDS).

ACROSS

1. TEN THOUSANDS

$$\begin{array}{r} 547 \\ \times\ 58 \\ \hline \end{array}$$

3. ONES

$$\begin{array}{r} 928 \\ \times\ 83 \\ \hline \end{array}$$

4. TEN THOUSANDS

$$\begin{array}{r} 670 \\ \times\ 39 \\ \hline \end{array}$$

5. HUNDREDS

$$\begin{array}{r} 779 \\ \times\ 60 \\ \hline \end{array}$$

8. THOUSANDS

$$\begin{array}{r} 706 \\ \times\ 90 \\ \hline \end{array}$$

9. HUNDREDS

$$\begin{array}{r} 623 \\ \times\ 74 \\ \hline \end{array}$$

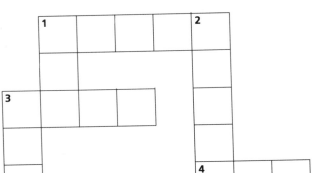
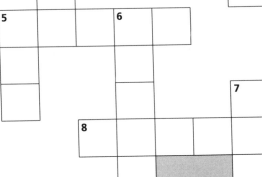

DOWN

1. THOUSANDS

$$\begin{array}{r} 981 \\ \times\ 64 \\ \hline \end{array}$$

2. HUNDREDS

$$\begin{array}{r} 378 \\ \times\ 34 \\ \hline \end{array}$$

3. THOUSANDS

$$\begin{array}{r} 820 \\ \times\ 55 \\ \hline \end{array}$$

5. HUNDREDS

$$\begin{array}{r} 786 \\ \times\ 25 \\ \hline \end{array}$$

6. TENS

$$\begin{array}{r} 805 \\ \times\ 76 \\ \hline \end{array}$$

7. TEN THOUSANDS

$$\begin{array}{r} 973 \\ \times\ 81 \\ \hline \end{array}$$

CROSS-NUMBER 15 PUZZLE

1 DIGIT X 3 DIGITS

Express each problem in its numerical form. Then solve the problems and write your answers in the appropriate across and down positions.

ACROSS

1. Multiply five hundred thirty-two by five.

2. Multiply three hundred twenty-six by eight.

4. Multiply eight hundred fifty-seven by two.

7. Multiply three hundred fifty-eight by nine.

10. Multiply five hundred nineteen by seven.

11. Multiply seven hundred by four.

DOWN

1. Multiply four hundred ninety by five.

3. Multiply two hundred nine by three.

5. Multiply five hundred ninety-nine by seven.

6. Multiply eight hundred eighty-four by three.

8. Multiply nine hundred one by three.

9. Multiply seven hundred twenty-three by six.

CROSS-NUMBER 16 PUZZLE

2 DIGITS X 2 DIGITS   Express each problem in its numerical form. Then solve the problems and write your answers in the appropriate across and down positions.

ACROSS

2. Multiply ninety-eight by seventy-four.

5. Multiply seventy-nine by forty-six.

7. Multiply eighty-four by seventy-six.

9. Multiply ninety-nine by twenty-eight.

10. Multiply forty-three by forty-two.

11. Multiply fifty-five by thirty-three.

DOWN

1. Multiply fifty-seven by thirty-eight.

2. Multiply ninety-two by eighty-four.

3. Multiply sixty-one by forty-seven.

4. Multiply thirty-seven by thirty-six.

6. Multiply seventy-two by fifty-nine.

8. Multiply sixty-six by fifty-three.

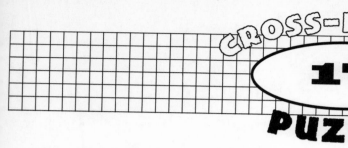

2 DIGITS X 3 DIGITS   Express each problem in its numerical form. Then solve the problems and write your answers in the appropriate across and down positions.

ACROSS

1. Multiply seven hundred nine by fifty-eight.

5. Multiply four hundred ninety-seven by sixty-four.

6. Multiply three hundred eighty by ninety-five.

9. Multiply five hundred two by thirty-seven.

10. Multiply nine hundred fifty by sixty-nine.

DOWN

2. Multiply five hundred seventy-four by thirty-seven.

3. Multiply four hundred fifty-one by twenty-six.

4. Multiply eight hundred four by eighty.

7. Multiply six hundred thirty-two by twenty-three.

8. Multiply six hundred seventy-three by forty.

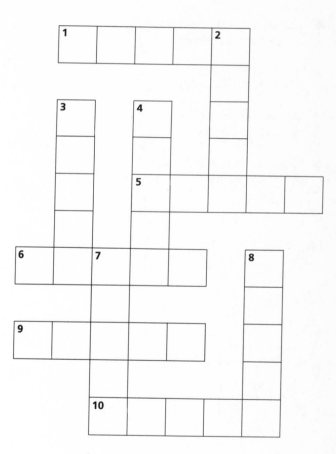

CROSS-NUMBER 18 PUZZLE

3 DIGITS X 3 DIGITS

Express each multiplication problem below in its numerical form. Then solve the problems and write your answers in the appropriate across and down positions.

ACROSS

2. Multiply seven hundred sixty-four by five hundred thirteen.

4. Multiply six hundred ninety-four by five hundred eighty.

5. Multiply three hundred by two hundred eighty.

8. Multiply seven hundred forty-nine by six hundred four.

9. Multiply five hundred nine by three hundred twenty.

DOWN

1. Multiply five hundred forty-seven by three hundred eighty-nine.

3. Multiply four hundred thirty-three by two hundred eight.

4. Multiply eight hundred fifteen by four hundred ninety-five.

6. Multiply six hundred ninety-eight by four hundred sixty-eight.

7. Multiply three hundred twenty-five by two hundred seventy-two.

NAME _____   DATE _____

D I V I S I O N

CROSS-NUMBER 19 PUZZLE

1-DIGIT DIVISOR, REMAINDERS Solve all of the problems below. If the answer to one of the problems has a remainder, fill in the answer as you would normally, then print an "R" in the tiny square followed by the remainder. For example, if your answer is 7765 remainder 8, do the following:

7 7 6 5 R 8

ACROSS

2. 7) 42,049   **4.** 5) 32,244

5. 3) 24,487   **7.** 4) 17,579

8. 2) 19,506   **11.** 6) 44,559

DOWN

1. 7) 33,576   **3.** 6) 33,636

5. 8) 65,472   **6.** 9) 21,635

9. 4) 28,170   **10.** 9) 16,002

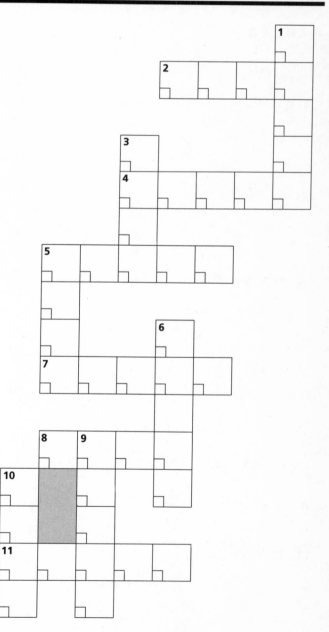

23

NAME _____   DATE _____

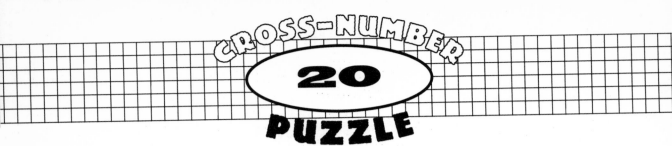

CROSS-NUMBER
20
PUZZLE

1-DIGIT DIVISOR, REMAINDERS Solve all of the division problems below. If the answer to one of your problems has a remainder, fill in the answer as you would normally, then print an "R" in the tiny square followed by the remainder.
For example, if your answer is 7765 remainder 8, do the following:

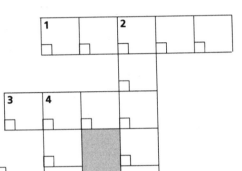

ACROSS

1. $44{,}845 \div 9 =$

3. $65{,}492 \div 7 =$

6. $79{,}210 \div 8 =$

7. $26{,}880 \div 5 =$

9. $25{,}223 \div 3 =$

11. $38{,}015 \div 5 =$

DOWN

2. $56{,}473 \div 7 =$

4. $7{,}522 \div 2 =$

5. $17{,}598 \div 6 =$

7. $20{,}241 \div 4 =$

8. $38{,}568 \div 6 =$

10. $56{,}078 \div 8 =$

CROSS-NUMBER 21 PUZZLE

2-DIGIT DIVISOR, REMAINDERS Solve all of the problems below. If the answer to one of the problems has a remainder, fill in the answer as you would normally, then print an "R" in the tiny square followed by the remainder. For example, if your answer is 7765 remainder 8, do the following:

| 7 | 7 | 6 | 5 | R 8 |

ACROSS

3. 68 ⟌ 66,912

4. 76 ⟌ 19,612

6. 63 ⟌ 31,941

7. 49 ⟌ 35,819

8. 24 ⟌ 8,856

10. 46 ⟌ 22,684

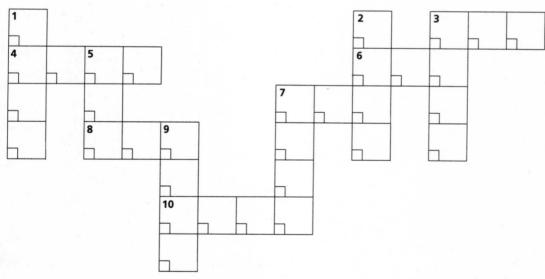

DOWN

1. 39 ⟌ 24,345

2. 72 ⟌ 61,280

3. 58 ⟌ 56,262

5. 50 ⟌ 40,150

7. 94 ⟌ 73,514

9. 73 ⟌ 67,459

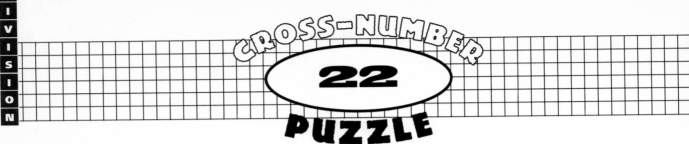

CROSS-NUMBER
22
PUZZLE

| **2-DIGIT DIVISOR, REMAINDERS** |

Solve all of the problems below. If the answer to one of the problems has a remainder, fill in the answer as you would normally, then print an "R" in the tiny square followed by the remainder. For example, if your answer is 7765 remainder 8, do the following:

ACROSS

1. 36,351 ÷ 54 =

4. 52,530 ÷ 53 =

6. 17,366 ÷ 80 =

8. 38,681 ÷ 47 =

10. 39,032 ÷ 68 =

11. 25,345 ÷ 37 =

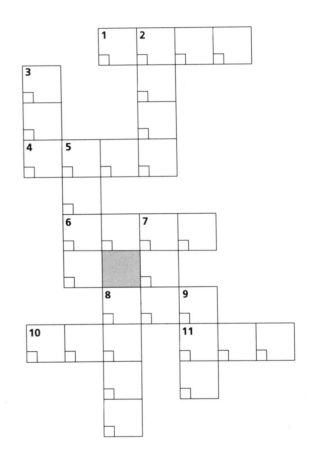

DOWN

2. 46,507 ÷ 62 =

3. 13,972 ÷ 28 =

5. 83,842 ÷ 89 =

7. 74,448 ÷ 94 =

8. 64,304 ÷ 76 =

9. 21,712 ÷ 59 =

CROSS-NUMBER 23 PUZZLE

3-DIGIT DIVISOR, REMAINDERS Solve all of the problems below. If the answer to one of the problems has a remainder, fill in the answer as you would normally, then print an "R" in the tiny square followed by the remainder. For example, if your answer is 7765 remainder 8, do the following:

| 7 | 7 | 6 | 5 | R 8 |

ACROSS

1. $477 \overline{) 284{,}299}$

2. $494 \overline{) 453{,}492}$

4. $911 \overline{) 410{,}861}$

5. $509 \overline{) 115{,}543}$

6. $708 \overline{) 512{,}592}$

8. $865 \overline{) 582{,}150}$

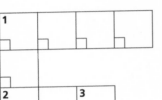
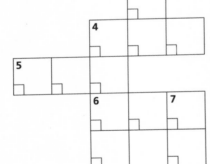
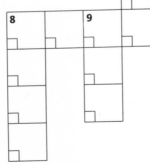

DOWN

1. $287 \overline{) 166{,}173}$

3. $558 \overline{) 449{,}190}$

4. $763 \overline{) 363{,}960}$

7. $700 \overline{) 309{,}405}$

8. $653 \overline{) 449{,}921}$

9. $717 \overline{) 272{,}460}$

CROSS-NUMBER 24 PUZZLE

3-DIGIT DIVISOR, REMAINDERS

Solve all of the problems below. If the answer to one of the problems has a remainder, fill in the answer as you would normally, then print an "R" in the tiny square followed by the remainder. For example, if your answer is 7765 remainder 8, do the following:

| 7 | 7 | 6 | 5 | R | 8 |

ACROSS

1. 153,462 ÷ 368 =

3. 401,868 ÷ 732 =

5. 595,350 ÷ 945 =

6. 609,966 ÷ 846 =

7. 240,093 ÷ 721 =

9. 301,087 ÷ 358 =

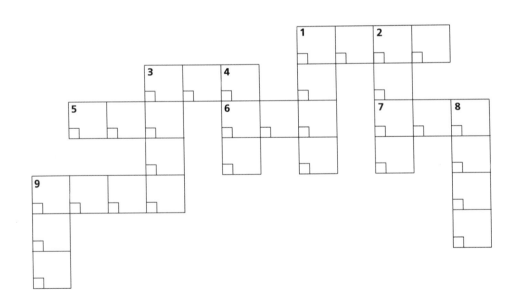

DOWN

1. 312,283 ÷ 636 =

2. 716,576 ÷ 927 =

3. 356,636 ÷ 709 =

4. 258,110 ÷ 265 =

8. 106,279 ÷ 326 =

9. 600,365 ÷ 719 =

NAME _____ DATE _____

CROSS-NUMBER
25
PUZZLE

1-DIGIT DIVISOR Solve the problems and write the answers in the appropriate across and down positions. The number you record in the outlined box shows where the letter should go in the code boxes at the bottom to solve the riddle.

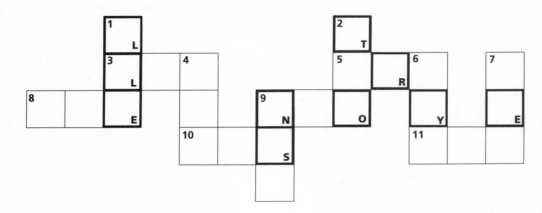

ACROSS

3. 8)‾4,296   **5.** 7)‾6,622   **8.** 4)‾2,692   **9.** 3)‾2,118   **10.** 2)‾1,642   **11.** 9)‾7,020

DOWN

1. 5)‾4,765   **2.** 8)‾2,368   **4.** 9)‾6,912   **6.** 7)‾4,249   **7.** 6)‾2,880   **9.** 9)‾6,471

What do you call a mean ogre who can't make friends?

MI | | | | | | | | | | | |
   | 1 | 2 | 3 | 4 | | 5 | 6 | 7 | 8 | 9 | 0 |

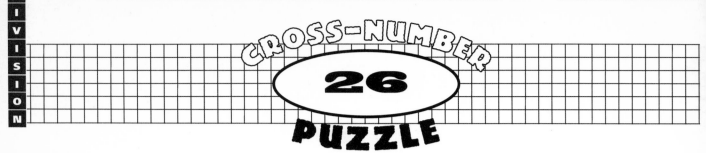

1-DIGIT DIVISOR

Solve the problems and write your answers in the appropriate across and down positions. The number you record in the outlined box shows where the letter should go in the code boxes at the bottom to solve the riddle.

ACROSS

2. 3,970 ÷ 5 =

4. 6,881 ÷ 7 =

6. 1,947 ÷ 3 =

7. 1,712 ÷ 2 =

8. 2,665 ÷ 5 =

10. 2,884 ÷ 4 =

DOWN

1. 3,816 ÷ 8 =

3. 2,933 ÷ 7 =

5. 2,034 ÷ 6 =

6. 1,815 ÷ 3 =

7. 4,938 ÷ 6 =

9. 3,123 ÷ 9 =

What goes tick tock croak, tick tock croak?

| 1 | | 2 | 3 | 4 | 5 | 6 | | 7 | 8 | 9 | 0 |

CROSS-NUMBER 27 PUZZLE

2-DIGIT DIVISOR Solve the problems and write your answers in the appropriate across and down positions. The number you record in the outlined box shows where the letter should go in the code boxes at the bottom to solve the riddle.

ACROSS

2. 61,504 ÷ 64 =

4. 49,518 ÷ 54 =

6. 42,570 ÷ 86 =

8. 28,413 ÷ 99 =

10. 49,104 ÷ 72 =

12. 31,320 ÷ 36 =

DOWN

1. 15,249 ÷ 39 =

3. 47,377 ÷ 73 =

5. 63,554 ÷ 86 =

7. 54,910 ÷ 95 =

9. 51,136 ÷ 68 =

11. 34,701 ÷ 43 =

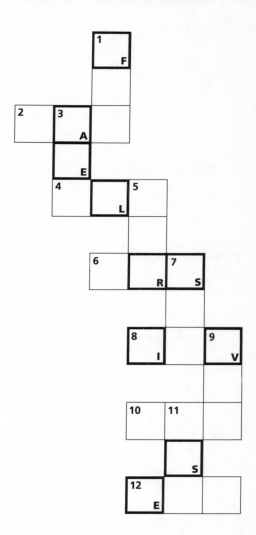

What did the daredevil eat before going over the waterfall in a barrel?

| | | | | | | | | | |
|1|2|3|4|5|6|7|8|9|0|

DIVISION

CROSS-NUMBER 28 PUZZLE

3-DIGIT DIVISOR Solve the problems below and write your answers in the appropriate across and down positions. The number you record in the outlined box shows where the letter should go in the code boxes at the bottom to solve the riddle.

ACROSS

1. 506) 486,772

3. 849) 674,106

5. 670) 546,050

8. 949) 576,992

9. 517) 474,089

11. 517) 229,031

DOWN

2. 476) 322,252

4. 776) 332,128

6. 791) 409,738

7. 838) 275,702

8. 300) 191,100

10. 643) 118,312

(Grid boxes: 1 I, 2 H; 3, 4; 5, 6 T, O; 7, 8, D; P; 9, 10, E; L; 11, N, E)

How do you get a swarm of bees out of an empty jar?

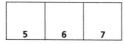
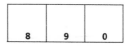

1 2 3 4   5 6 7   8 9 0

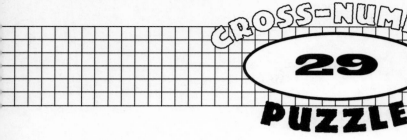

CROSS-NUMBER **29** PUZZLE

1-DIGIT DIVISOR: ONES THROUGH THOUSANDS   Solve the problems below. Study your answer and fill in the puzzle by spelling out the number found in the indicated place value column (ONES, TENS, HUNDREDS, or THOUSANDS).

ACROSS

1. THOUSANDS
$49,668 \div 6 =$

3. ONES
$35,946 \div 9 =$

4. HUNDREDS
$38,535 \div 5 =$

6. ONES
$16,989 \div 3 =$

8. THOUSANDS
$38,976 \div 8 =$

10. HUNDREDS
$58,518 \div 6 =$

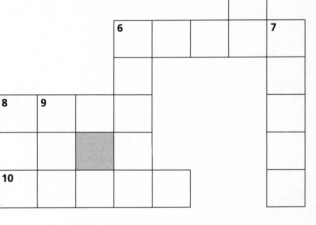

DOWN

2. ONES
$24,608 \div 4 =$

3. TENS
$24,224 \div 4 =$

5. THOUSANDS
$65,415 \div 7 =$

6. TENS
$14,872 \div 2 =$

7. THOUSANDS
$40,450 \div 5 =$

9. HUNDREDS
$15,582 \div 3 =$

CROSS-NUMBER 30 PUZZLE

1-DIGIT DIVISOR, ONES THROUGH THOUSANDS

Solve the problems below. Study your answer and fill in the puzzle by spelling out the number found in the indicated place value column (ONES, TENS, HUNDREDS, or THOUSANDS).

ACROSS

2. HUNDREDS 84) 714,420

4. THOUSANDS 58) 172,492

5. ONES 79) 404,243

9. THOUSANDS 97) 331,934

10. HUNDREDS 52) 412,672

11. TENS 37) 236,356

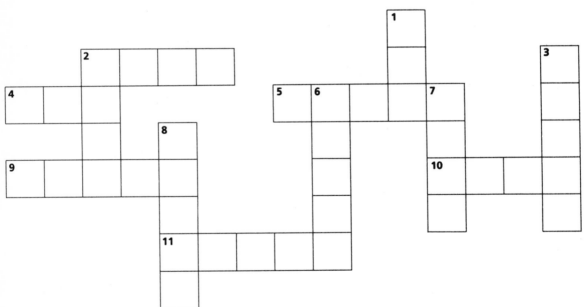

DOWN

1. HUNDREDS 80) 730,960

2. THOUSANDS 76) 310,916

3. TENS 43) 252,410

6. ONES 46) 133,768

7. HUNDREDS 24) 237,600

8. THOUSANDS 72) 504,504

CROSS-NUMBER
31
PUZZLE

1-DIGIT DIVISION Express each problem in its numerical form. Then solve the problems and write your answers in the appropriate across and down positions.

ACROSS

1. Divide three thousand nine hundred twenty by five.

2. Divide four thousand seven hundred thirty by five.

5. Divide five thousand two hundred fifty by seven.

7. Divide two thousand four hundred twenty-four by six.

8. Divide three thousand three hundred by four.

10. Divide one thousand seven hundred nineteen by nine.

DOWN

1. Divide four thousand three hundred seventy-four by six.

3. Divide five thousand five hundred fifty-three by nine.

4. Divide one thousand four hundred by two.

6. Divide one thousand seven hundred fifty-two by three.

7. Divide three thousand nine hundred thirty-six by eight.

9. Divide four thousand five hundred sixty-eight by eight.

CROSS-NUMBER 32 PUZZLE

Express each problem in its numerical form. Then solve the problems and write your answers in the appropriate across and down positions.

ACROSS

1. Divide fourteen thousand seven hundred thirty-six by forty-eight.

2. Divide sixty-eight thousand nine hundred eight by ninety-two.

3. Divide twenty-seven thousand six hundred forty-eight by thirty-two.

5. Divide fifty thousand five hundred sixteen by seventy-three.

7. Divide thirty-four thousand four hundred eighty-five by fifty-seven.

9. Divide thirty thousand five hundred ninety by thirty-eight.

DOWN

1. Divide thirty thousand three hundred twenty-four by seventy-six.

2. Divide thirty-two thousand four hundred seventy-two by forty-four.

4. Divide thirty-nine thousand one hundred seventy-six by eighty-three.

6. Divide eighty-one thousand four hundred thirty-two by eighty-seven.

8. Divide fifty-one thousand nine hundred forty by ninety-eight.

9. Divide fifty-six thousand by sixty-four.

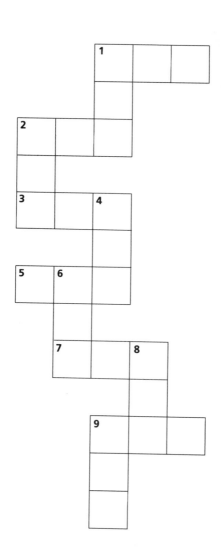

| 3-DIGIT DIVISION | Express each problem in its numerical form. Then solve the problems and write your answers in the appropriate across and down positions. |

ACROSS

2. Divide two hundred seventy-three thousand, three hundred eighty-five by three hundred sixty-five.

6. Divide two hundred eight thousand, two hundred fifty-one by two hundred forty-three.

9. Divide six hundred thirty-eight thousand, four hundred ninety-six by seven hundred thirty-nine.

3. Divide six hundred ninety-five thousand, one hundred thirty by nine hundred eighty-six.

7. Divide six hundred sixty-eight thousand, two hundred eighty-eight by nine hundred eight.

10. Divide six hundred forty-six thousand, five hundred eighty-one by eight hundred forty-three.

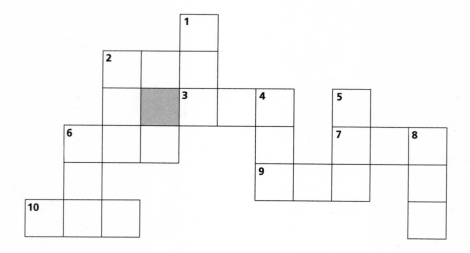

DOWN

1. Divide one hundred seventy-eight thousand, two hundred by six hundred.

4. Divide three hundred ninety-eight thousand, eight hundred twenty by six hundred ninety.

6. Divide two hundred sixty-five thousand, eight hundred by three hundred.

2. Divide three hundred forty-eight thousand, two hundred ten by four hundred thirty-eight.

5. Divide three hundred sixty-six thousand, two hundred twelve by six hundred thirty-eight.

8. Divide five hundred fifty-one thousand, fifty-one by eight hundred fifty-seven.

NAME _____   DATE _____

| 1-DIGIT DIVISOR, REMAINDERS | Solve the problems below. Each answer has a remainder. Write the remainder in words in the puzzle. |

ACROSS

1. $1,836 \div 7 =$

3. $2,759 \div 6 =$

4. $4,197 \div 5 =$

5. $3,407 \div 8 =$

7. $4,366 \div 7 =$

8. $3,091 \div 4 =$

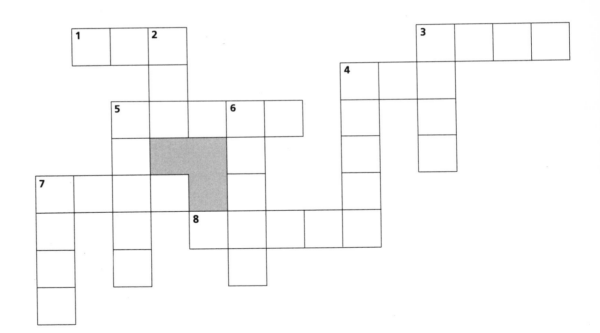

DOWN

2. $2,062 \div 3 =$

3. $2,636 \div 7 =$

4. $2,933 \div 5 =$

5. $5,695 \div 8 =$

6. $4,526 \div 9 =$

7. $1,750 \div 6 =$

CROSS-NUMBER 35 PUZZLE

2-DIGIT DIVISOR, REMAINDERS

Solve the problems below. Each answer has a remainder. Write the remainder in words in the puzzle.

ACROSS

1. $59 \overline{)45,519}$

3. $44 \overline{)29,969}$

4. $45 \overline{)22,338}$

7. $37 \overline{)35,091}$

9. $49 \overline{)24,855}$

DOWN

1. $84 \overline{)52,923}$

2. $65 \overline{)48,042}$

5. $89 \overline{)39,163}$

6. $64 \overline{)51,698}$

8. $28 \overline{)9,360}$

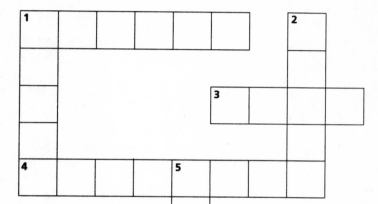

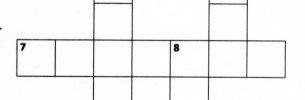

CROSS-NUMBER 36 PUZZLE

3-DIGIT DIVISOR, REMAINDERS

Solve the problems below. Each answer has a remainder. Write the remainder in words in the puzzle.

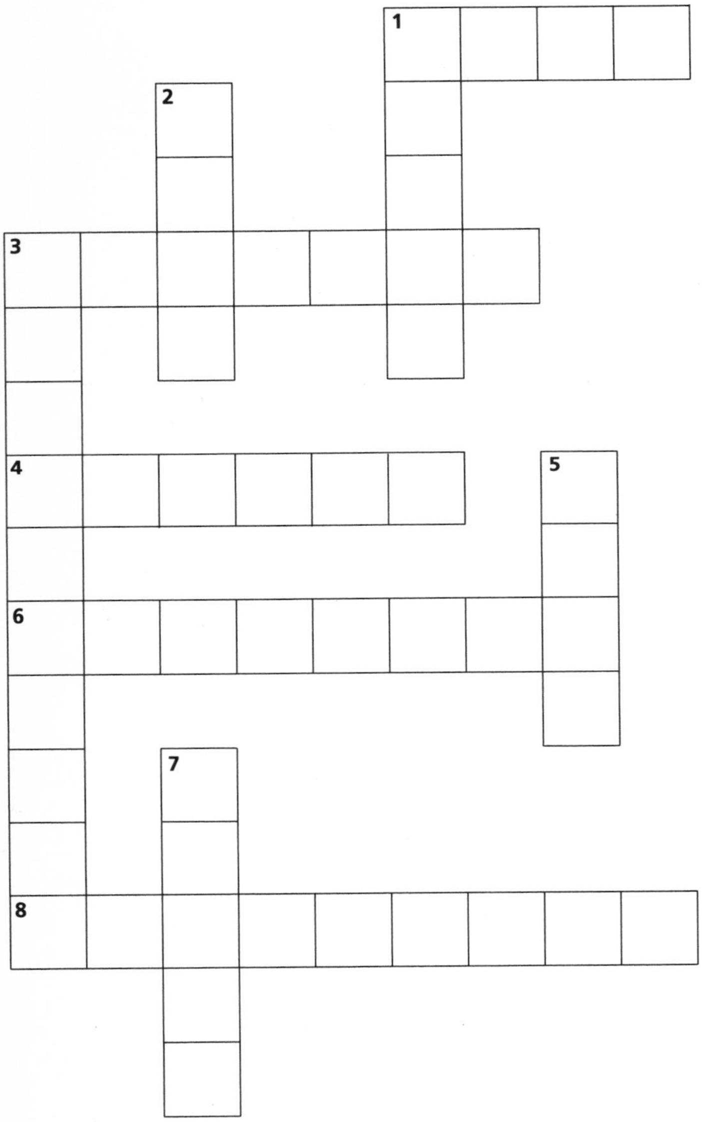

ACROSS

1. 322,384 ÷ 597 =

3. 224,926 ÷ 347 =

4. 151,060 ÷ 590 =

6. 453,829 ÷ 792 =

8. 129,859 ÷ 347 =

DOWN

1. 566,725 ÷ 771 =

2. 477,703 ÷ 494 =

3. 191,905 ÷ 386 =

5. 542,019 ÷ 890 =

7. 652,120 ÷ 769 =

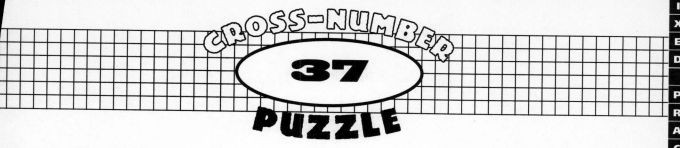

1-DIGIT FACTORS OR DIVISORS, REMAINDERS

Solve all of the problems below. If the answer to one of the division problems has a remainder, fill in the answer as you would normally, then print an "R" in the tiny square followed by the remainder. For example, if your answer is 7765 remainder 8, do the following:

7	7	6	5	R8

ACROSS

1. $5{,}984 \times 6 =$

3. $8{,}309 \times 7 =$

4. $4{,}743 \div 6 =$

7. $471 \times 8 =$

8. $5{,}070 \times 3 =$

9. $3{,}279 \div 8 =$

DOWN

1. $639 \times 5 =$

2. $26{,}551 \div 4 =$

5. $852{,}506 \div 9 =$

6. $1{,}894 \div 5 =$

7. $661 \times 5 =$

8. $5{,}524 \div 5 =$

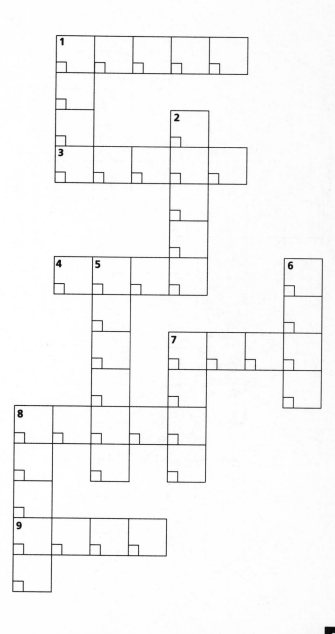

CROSS-NUMBER 38 PUZZLE

2-DIGIT FACTORS OR DIVISORS, REMAINDERS

Solve all of the problems below. If the answer to one of the division problems has a remainder, fill in the answer as you would normally, then print an "R" in the tiny square followed by the remainder. For example, if your answer is 7765 remainder 8, do the following:

| 7 | 7 | 6 | 5 | R8 |

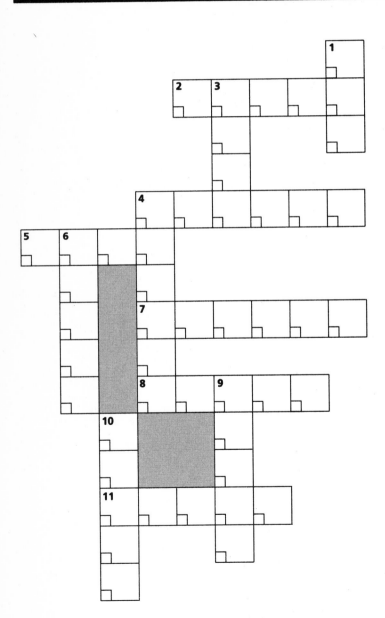

ACROSS

2. 691 × 75 =

4. 2,037 × 60 =

5. 57 × 45 =

7. 560,765 ÷ 64 =

8. 54,524 ÷ 81 =

11. 434,740 ÷ 48 =

DOWN

1. 3,379 ÷ 75 =

3. 83 × 24 =

4. 3,476 × 46 =

6. 40,420 ÷ 74 =

9. 328 × 92 =

10. 28,454 ÷ 57 =

CROSS-NUMBER 39 PUZZLE

3-DIGIT FACTORS OR DIVISORS, REMAINDERS Solve all of the problems below. If the answer to one of the division problems has a remainder, fill in the answer as you would normally, then print an "R" in the tiny square followed by the remainder. For example, if your answer is 7765 remainder 8, do the following:

7 7 6 5 [R] 8

ACROSS

2. 626,588 ÷ 708 =

4. 333 × 403 =

5. 541 × 330 =

7. 643 × 251 =

10. 342,730 ÷ 408 =

11. 17,282 ÷ 351 =

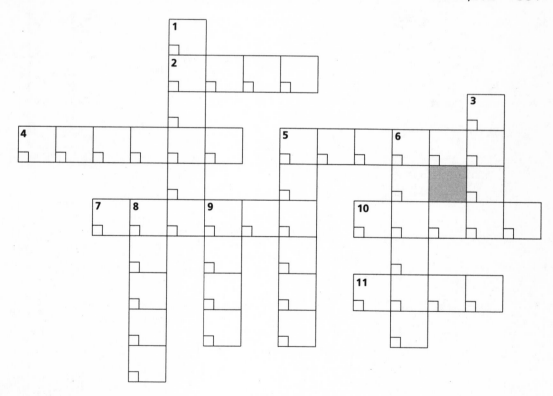

DOWN

1. 747 × 253 =

3. 174,070 ÷ 567 =

5. 598 × 274 =

6. 784 × 694 =

8. 158,491 ÷ 248 =

9. 17,952 ÷ 472 =

MIXED PRACTICE

CROSS-NUMBER 40 PUZZLE

MIXED OPERATIONS, REMAINDERS Solve all of the problems below. If the answer to one of the division problems has a remainder, fill in the answer as you would normally, then print an "R" in the tiny square followed by the remainder. For example, if your answer is 7765 remainder 8, do the following:

| 7 | 7 | 6 | 5 | R 8 |

ACROSS

1. $3,689 \div 4 =$

3. $69 \times 35 =$

5. $230,148 \div 84 =$

8. $550 \times 409 =$

9. $385 \times 79 =$

10. $15,961 \div 2 =$

DOWN

1. $39,949 \div 42 =$

2. $481 \times 229 =$

4. $4,903 \times 8 =$

5. $162,514 \div 663 =$

6. $343,091 \div 360 =$

7. $763 \times 6 =$

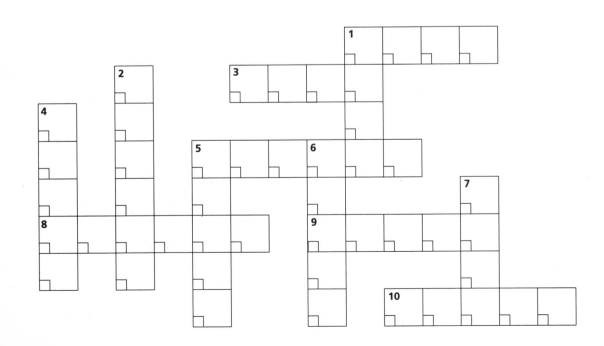

ANSWER KEY

Puzzle #1
ACROSS
1. 2,905
4. 3,576
7. 6,951
9. 7,632
10. 6,435
11. 4,160
DOWN
1. 2,034
2. 5,682
3. 876
5. 5,454
6. 6,776
8. 1,131

Puzzle #2
ACROSS
1. 4,275
3. 3,024
5. 1,682
7. 1,938
8. 4,774
10. 5,052
12. 1,902
DOWN
2. 5,728
3. 3,546
4. 3,168
6. 2,187
9. 4,780
10. 5,772
11. 2,192

Puzzle #3
ACROSS
2. 71,488
3. 58,849
6. 22,290
7. 11,752
9. 67,689
11. 21,775
DOWN
1. 38,592
4. 81,720
5. 10,012

8. 18,147
9. 66,129
10. 9,835

Puzzle #4
ACROSS
2. 2,124
3. 7,802
5. 8,624
7. 2,156
9. 4,029
11. 4,020
13. 1,265
DOWN
1. 2,847
2. 2,268
4. 2,115
6. 6,290
8. 6,750
10. 2,516
12. 2,400

Puzzle #5
ACROSS
2. 18,944
5. 11,232
6. 27,306
8. 60,228
9. 56,924
10. 77,670
DOWN
1. 12,154
2. 18,308
3. 47,550
4. 37,370
6. 26,712
7. 22,750

Puzzle #6
ACROSS
3. 15,561
5. 36,736
7. 27,782
9. 26,400
11. 45,496
12. 14,280

DOWN
1. 31,770
2. 21,088
4. 53,392
6. 28,500
8. 25,636
10. 47,424

Puzzle #7
ACROSS
1. 373,230
3. 431,120
8. 105,252
9. 307,877
10. 202,730
11. 715,572
DOWN
2. 291,648
3. 491,841
4. 125,112
5. 138,040
6. 211,765
7. 687,892

Puzzle #8
ACROSS
2. 222,768
4. 669,342
6. 652,878
9. 318,936
10. 616,896
11. 320,450
DOWN
1. 89,401
2. 248,576
3. 831,296
5. 758,520
7. 231,030
8. 198,791

Puzzle #9
ACROSS
1. 185,436
4. 393,540
6. 466,320
8. 264,264
10. 766,213
11. 186,750

DOWN
2. 536,537
3. 490,203
5. 503,440
6. 436,455
7. 272,663
9. 69,861

Puzzle #10
ACROSS
1. 1,652
5. 4,350
6. 4,856
9. 6,464
10. 3,486
11. 4,858
DOWN
1. 1,476
2. 2,844
3. 7,496
4. 2,093
7. 5,124
8. 4,428

What can't you give a person who has laughed his head off?
A BAD HEADACHE

Puzzle #11
ACROSS
2. 30,240
3. 40,280
5. 41,503
7. 23,750
8. 77,265
11. 14,688
DOWN
1. 55,232
2. 38,900
4. 28,153
6. 31,095
9. 69,336
10. 10,846

How do you contact giant squid?
DROP THEM A LINE

Puzzle #12
ACROSS
1. 378,324
4. 513,864
7. 667,200
8. 220,817
9. 532,560
10. 339,010
DOWN
2. 350,400
3. 454,960
4. 542,256
5. 382,226
6. 468,600
7. 678,388

What runs around a graveyard but does not move?
A STURDY FENCE

Puzzle #13
ACROSS
1. 1,482; eight
4. 2,436; four
6. 4,679; seven
8. 3,551; three
9. 928; two
10. 1,026; zero
DOWN
2. 4,543; three
3. 8,277; eight
4. 3,584; five
5. 1,776; one
7. 5,985; nine
9. 5,293; two

Puzzle #14
ACROSS
1. 31,726; three
3. 77,024; four
4. 26,130; two
5. 46,740; seven
8. 63,540; three
9. 46,102; one

DOWN
1. 62,784; two
2. 12,852; eight
3. 45,100; five
5. 19,650; six
6. 61,180; eight
7. 78,813; seven

Puzzle #15
ACROSS
1. 2,660
2. 2,608
4. 1,714
7. 3,222
10. 3,633
11. 2,800
DOWN
1. 2,450
3. 627
5. 4,193
6. 2,652
8. 2,703
9. 4,338

Puzzle #16
ACROSS
2. 7,252
5. 3,634
7. 6,384
9. 2,772
10. 1,806
11. 1,815
DOWN
1. 2,166
2. 7,728
3. 2,867
4. 1,332
6. 4,248
8. 3,498

Puzzle #17
ACROSS
1. 41,122
5. 31,808
6. 36,100
9. 18,574
10. 65,550

DOWN
2. 21,238
3. 11,726
4. 64,320
7. 14,536
8. 26,920

Puzzle #18
ACROSS
2. 391,932
4. 402,520
5. 84,000
8. 452,396
9. 162,880
DOWN
1. 212,783
3. 90,064
4. 403,425
6. 326,664
7. 88,400

Puzzle #19
ACROSS
2. 6,007
4. 6,448 R4
5. 8,162 R1
7. 4,394 R3
8. 9,753
11. 7,426 R3
DOWN
1. 4,796 R4
3. 5,606
5. 8,184
6. 2,403 R8
9. 7,042 R2
10. 1,778

Puzzle #20
ACROSS
1. 4,982 R7
3. 9,356
6. 9,901 R2
7. 5,376
9. 8,407 R2
11. 7,603

DOWN
2. 8,067 R4
4. 3,761
5. 2,933
7. 5,060 R1
8. 6,428
10. 7,009 R6

Puzzle #21
ACROSS
3. 984
4. 258 R4
6. 507
7. 731
8. 369
10. 493 R6
DOWN
1. 624 R9
2. 851 R8
3. 970 R2
5. 803
7. 782 R6
9. 924 R7

Puzzle #22
ACROSS
1. 673 R9
4. 991 R7
6. 217 R6
8. 823
10. 574
11. 685
DOWN
2. 750 R7
3. 499
5. 942 R4
7. 792
8. 846 R8
9. 368

Puzzle #23
ACROSS
1. 596 R7
2. 918
4. 451
5. 227
6. 724
8. 673 R5

OWN
1. 579
3. 805
4. 477 R9
7. 442 R5
8. 689 R4
9. 380

Puzzle #24
ACROSS
1. 417 R6
3. 549
5. 630
6. 721
7. 333
9. 841 R9
DOWN
1. 491 R7
2. 773 R5
3. 503 R9
4. 974
8. 326 R3
9. 835

Puzzle #25
ACROSS
3. 537
5. 946
8. 673
9. 706
10. 821
11. 780
DOWN
1. 953
2. 296
4. 768
6. 607
7. 480
9. 719
*What do you call a
mean ogre who can't
make friends?*
MISTER LONELY

Puzzle #26
ACROSS
2. 794
4. 983
6. 649
7. 856
8. 533
10. 721
DOWN
1. 477
3. 419
5. 339
6. 605
7. 823
9. 347
*What goes tick tock
croak, tick tock croak?*
A WATCH FROG

Puzzle #27
ACROSS
2. 961
4. 917
6. 495
8. 287
10. 682
12. 870
DOWN
1. 391
3. 649
5. 739
7. 578
9. 752
11. 807
*What did the daredevil
eat before going over
the waterfall in a barrel?*
LIFESAVERS

Puzzle #28
ACROSS
1. 962
3. 794
5. 815
8. 608
9. 917
11. 443

DOWN
2. 677
4. 428
6. 518
7. 329
8. 637
10. 184
*How do you get a
swarm of bees out of
an empty jar?*
OPEN THE LID

Puzzle #29
ACROSS
1. 8,278; eight
3. 3,994; four
4. 7,707; seven
6. 5,663; three
8. 4,872; four
10. 9,753; seven
DOWN
2. 6,152; two
3. 6,056; five
5. 9,345; nine
6. 7,436; three
7. 8,090; eight
9. 5,194; one

Puzzle #30
ACROSS
2. 8,505; five
4. 2,974; two
5. 5,117; seven
9. 3,422; three
10. 7,936; nine
11. 6,388; eight
DOWN
1. 9,137; one
2. 4,091; four
3. 5,870; seven
6. 2,908; eight
7. 9,900; nine
8. 7,007; seven

Puzzle #31
ACROSS
1. 784
2. 946
5. 750
7. 404
8. 825
10. 191
DOWN
1. 729
3. 617
4. 700
6. 584
7. 492
9. 571

Puzzle #32
ACROSS
1. 307
2. 749
3. 864
5. 692
7. 605
9. 805
DOWN
1. 399
2. 738
4. 472
6. 936
8. 530
9. 875

Puzzle #33
ACROSS
2. 749
3. 705
6. 857
7. 736
9. 864
10. 767
DOWN
1. 297
2. 795
4. 578
5. 574
6. 886
8. 643

Puzzle #34
ACROSS
1. 262 R2; two
3. 459 R5; five
4. 839 R2; two
5. 425 R7; seven
7. 623 R5; five
8. 772 R3; three
DOWN
2. 687 R1; one
3. 376 R4; four
4. 586 R3; three
5. 711 R7; seven
6. 502 R8; eight
7. 291 R4; four

Puzzle #35
ACROSS
1. 771 R30; thirty
3. 681 R5; five
4. 496 R18; eighteen
7. 948 R15; fifteen
9. 507 R12; twelve
DOWN
1. 630 R3; three
2. 739 R7; seven
5. 440 R3; three
6. 807 R50; fifty
8. 334 R8; eight

Puzzle #36
ACROSS
1. four
3. seventy
4. twenty
6. thirteen
8. eighty-one
DOWN
1. forty
2. five
3. sixty-three
5. nine
7. eight

Puzzle #37
ACROSS
1. 35,904
3. 58,163
4. 790 R3
7. 3,768
8. 15,210
9. 409 R7
DOWN
1. 3,195
2. 6,637 R3
5. 94,722 R8
6. 378 R4
7. 3,305
8. 1,104 R4

Puzzle #38
ACROSS
2. 51,825
4. 122,220
5. 2,565
7. 8,761 R61
8. 673 R11
11. 9,057 R4
DOWN
1. 45 R4
3. 1,992
4. 159,896
6. 546 R16
9. 30,176
10. 499 R11

Puzzle #39
ACROSS
2. 885 R8
4. 134,199
5. 178,530
7. 161,393
10. 840 R10
11. 49 R83
DOWN
1. 188,991
3. 307 R1
5. 163,852
6. 544,096
8. 639 R19
9. 38 R16

Puzzle #40
ACROSS
1. 922 R1
3. 2,415
5. 2,739 R72
8. 224,950
9. 30,415
10. 7,980 R1
DOWN
1. 951 R7
2. 110,149
4. 39,224
5. 245 R79
6. 953 R11
7. 4,578